Early Praise for TACKL

Julia Hubbel's simple, to-the-point book covers the essence of good salesmanship at any level, but especially how to sell to major corporations. This concise book should be in every salesperson's briefcase.

> — Dr. Tony Alessandra, author of *Non-Manipulative Selling* and *The Platinum Rule for Sales Mastery*

This book will make you much more confident and comfortable dealing with the big deals. It's a quick read, but take your time. You will want to digest and use these insights.

> — Jim Cathcart, author of *Relationship Selling*

Guerrillas always make their message memorable. Julia shows you how. Every salesperson should read this book!

> — Orvel Ray Wilson, CSP, author of *Guerrilla Selling* author and speaker

A concise and compelling look at how to show value and land business.

> — Randy Gage, author of *Prosperity Mind*

Strong practical advice and guidance on how best to present yourself, your company, and your products and services from a successful international entrepreneur. Excellent tools to arm yourself for *Tackling the Titans*!

> — Pamela A. Prince-Eason, President and CEO, Women's Business Enterprise National Council

An insightful look at sales in the 21st century. Refresh your outlook with these proven strategies and techniques to sustain and grow a successful business!

— Dr. Nido Qubein, President, High Point University: Chairman, Great Harvest Bread Co.

Julia doesn't mince words when she gives advice on what to do and what to avoid. This is a great book on getting business in the real world. It can benefit any person — minority or not — who wants to excel in business.

— Terry L. Brock, MBA, CSP, CPAE

It is often said that knowledge is power. . . .Well, the practical knowledge you will gain from reading *Tackling the Titans* will make the engaged user powerful indeed!

— John Taylor, Manager, Supplier Diversity Development Global Supply Chain, Delphi Corporation

This book clearly defines simple principles that can be used to improve a company's strategy and impact in presenting to major corporations.

— Donovan Casanave, MBA, Supplier Diversity Leader, Shell Oil

TACKLING THE TITANS

HOW TO SELL TO THE FORTUNE 500

A Guide for Diverse and Veteran Suppliers

JULIA HUBBEL

The Hubbel Group Inc.

Most of the stories and examples in this book are true. In some instances, the names of people have been changed to protect their identity.

Requests for permission to make copies of any part of the work should be submitted to the publisher at The Hubbel Group, Inc.

Edited by Barbara Munson, www.MunsonCommunications.com

Cover design and interior page layout by Kerrie Lian, under contract with MacGraphics Services: www.MacGraphics.net

Printed in the United States of America.

First edition

ISBN: 978-0-9828631-1-4

Library of Congress Control Number: 2011904980

The Hubbel Group, Inc.
P.O. Box 27352
Lakewood, CO 80227
www.TheHUBFactor.com
720.221.7335

Dedication

This little book is dedicated to the talented and capable community of supplier diversity professionals who have opened the doors of their companies to the women, minorities, and veterans who seek to do business with them.

It is dedicated to everyone who ever gave me a shot, a chance, an opportunity. Who taught me about what service really is, and what it takes to earn the right to do business with America's giant corporations.

It is dedicated to the men and women who answer the phones, travel to the conferences, and constantly make the case every single day for those of us who just want that one meeting. May we make them proud, live up to their expectations, and remind them of how much we appreciate their efforts. Without them, most of us would never have these companies on our client lists.

Foreword

By Dave Nelson, CPM, Dave Nelson Group, Inc.

People who have worked in the purchasing function for years, as I have, meet hundreds, if not thousands, of salespeople who are trying to get us to buy their products or services. Some of these salespeople are outstanding, and do just about everything right. But there are so many—most, I would say—who do a poor job of presenting themselves, their company, or their products. This is sad because it is human nature to want to do a good job; they just need some guidance.

As I read through *Tackling the Titans*, I could see why so many people don't do such a good job. This book nails many of the problems that we all see as we deal with salespeople almost every day. You may recognize some of the mistakes you have been making and been unaware of until now. The book will be valuable to suppliers, in any industry, at any level, no matter how long they've been in business. In fact, the longer that people are in business, the harder it is for them to explain what they do. They get so complacent about their business, they lose clarity and edge.

Reading this book makes me want to buy a bunch of copies to hand them out to the sales folks I meet, and say to them, "Here, take this book home and read it tonight." If I were running a sales department, I would definitely give this book to everyone in the department and tell them, "This is how I want you to sell, and if you cannot follow these suggestions, then go sell for someone else, preferably our competitor."

I'll go a step further. Not only should salespeople read this book, we all should, because we often are selling our ideas to others. I just read this book for the first time two weeks ago, and I'm certain that I've already made several improvements. So, read it and think about some of the things you can improve when selling or presenting your ideas to others. The techniques in this book do not take away your own unique approach. They simply point out the common mistakes that many of us may make.

The global reach of this book really hit me when I was recently called on to help an old friend. He asked if I could get him an audience with key players at Honda to introduce a unique product. I drove up to Marysville, Ohio, and met with several Honda people, who used to work for me but are now all grown up. I have to say my friend was the epitome of the salespeople described in this book. First, Honda did not buy the kind of products he was selling, but some of their suppliers do. Second, Honda does not dictate who those suppliers should buy from. My friend had not done even the most basic research. Yes, he had a great product, but he didn't have a plan or a presentation prepared, and the story goes on and on. I sent him a long letter, put in a nice way, which gave him a bunch of pointers, just like those in this book.

I was recently on a conference call with key guys from Delphi purchasing because two friends of mine had an important meeting with them. John Wu owns an MBE business in Troy, Michigan, where Delphi's headquarters are located. About three months earlier, his mother-in-law, a Chinese woman named Madam Li, called and said that a real good friend of hers had started a business several years ago in electronics (with one machine set up in his living room). The business had now grown to $150 million revenue annually. In China they sell Delphi $6 million worth of products, have a record for perfect delivery and quality, and have won many awards from companies like Siemens, Bosch, Leer, JCI as well as the OEs. Madam Li wondered if I would ask Delphi to allow them to quote on and get some pilot orders for them from Delphi in the United States. So I did, and that is the process that they are going through right now. Her son-in-law is an ex-GM purchasing guy, has worked for other major companies, and, for the past six or eight years, has developed a very successful business selling chemicals, pharmaceuticals, and a few other things that Madam Li arranges to be made and shipped from China, through John Wu's MBE business. He sells them all over North and South America. He is good and he is smart, but he will be smarter when he reads this book.

More and more the world is shrinking. But we need to keep in mind that getting business at Honda, Toyota, or Nissan is still different than getting business from a traditional Western supplier. One thing that is true anywhere in the world is that buyers are motivated to give new business opportunities for many different reasons, and the more you know about what motivates the buyers who you call on, the better your chances of getting an RFQ or future business. This book gives you the tools to do just that.

Acknowledgments

In particular, thanks go to Shelley Stewart of Tyco International, without whose support and mentoring I'd never have gotten certified and had these doors opened for my company. Shelley, you are head and shoulders above us all. Keep on doing what you're doing.

To Michael Robinson, Program Director, Global Supplier Diversity IBM, for his excellent input and wise counsel on this manuscript, and for his ongoing leadership in the field of supplier diversity. You are the best.

To John Taylor, Delphi Corporation, for his careful review and excellent suggestions. Thank you for your friendship and your contributions to the field. We all love you. Thanks to Joan Kerr, Director of Supplier Diversity and Supplier Development at Pacific Gas & Electric, for her kind review and blessing of this book.

Thank you to Theresa Harrison, an outstanding leader in the field of supplier diversity, for her review and wise comments.

To the women of WBENC, whose organization makes so much possible for so many women entrepreneurs. Never stop what you're doing; we need you.

To NMSDC, the organization that set the bar for helping minorities conduct business with corporate America. It's a joy to work with the Councils.

To the many, many veterans' organizations, including NAVO-BA, that fight to help veterans get back to work and contributing to this great country.

To all the many talented supplier diversity professionals who have taught me over the years and who have provided input and stories for this book, thank you.

To the National Gay and Lesbian Chamber of Commerce for opening the doors to corporate America.

To the US Business Leadership Network for creating opportunities for the disabled to contribute their skills, knowledge and competence.

Contents

Introduction 11

The Challenge You Face 13

Find Your Niche 15

Don't Paper the Universe 17

Know When to Say When 19

Assessing Yourself: A Decision Tree 20

"So, what do you guys do?" 21

"I'm an MBE/WBE, and I'm looking for opportunities." 23

"Just tell me what you want done, and I can do it." 24

"I can help you meet your supplier diversity goals." 26

Advocates 27

Simplicity and Clarity 28

The Train Wreck 30

It's a Small World 32

Benefit of the Doubt 34

"I'm a minority/woman business owner and you *have*
    to do business with me." 35

"I'm not leaving until you give me some business." 36

Your Seven-Second First Impression 38

Your Value Proposition 40

Start with Research 41

Keep the Proposition Sticky and Simple 42

Value Proposition Examples 44

A Word on Multiple Value Propositions 46

Writing Your Value Proposition 47

Choose Your Words with Care 48

What to Cut from Your Value Proposition 50

More Examples 51

Your Capability Statement... 52

Developing Your Capability Statement 54

If You're Brand New 58

Creating Collaborations 58

This May Not Be Your Market 60

Strategic Networking.. 61

Network in Your NAICS Code 62

Check the Community 63

A Word on Networking 64

You're On, 24/7 66

Don't Be Addicted to Your Logo 68

Business School Programs.. 69

It Takes Time... 71

Know the SD Ropes.. 74

Spread It Around 76

Matchmakers... 78

About the Competition.. 80

Show Your Expertise 81

Words They Love to Hear... 82

Staying in Touch 83

Your Business Plan...Create a New Vision 84

Your Finances.. 86

Your Supporting Cast... 87

Time to Give Back.. 89

Tackling the Titans Success Checklist............................ 90

About the Author 91

Introduction

By applying the principles and lessons found in this book you can vastly improve your chances of doing business with America's major corporations *if you have a product or service that fits their needs.*

Imagine that you've been standing in line at WBENC or NMSDC, waiting for a chance to talk to Sheila Bright, a Supplier Diversity Professional at AT&T. A dozen people are behind you, also waiting to talk to Sheila. The guy in line ahead of you steps up to her. In a couple of minutes, it will be your turn, and you can feel the pressure. It's like a spotlight is on, and now it's his big moment. You listen in as Sheila shakes his hand and says, "What do you do?"

And all the guy says is, "I'm an MBE, and I'm looking for opportunities."

Or, "I can help you meet your supplier diversity goals."

Or maybe, "I'm a minority-owned business and you *have* to do business with me."

Or just, "We do I.T."

Or he has the nerve to say, "Just tell me what you want done, and I can do it."

Or he proves himself a complete idiot by asking, "So, what do you guys do?"

These are just some of the opening gambits we've heard Minority and Women Business Enterprise (MWBE) owners and reps use to ensure that the door to business opportunities will be slammed shut.

MWBEs, LGBTs close their businesses down for a week, pay thousands of dollars to attend a national conference, spend hours on their feet just for the chance to get in front of hundreds of Fortune 500 corporations. It's a big investment, but they get real face time with their Supplier Diversity (SD) professionals, sent there to help bridge the opportunities gap. Then these MWBEs systematically ruin their chances by making statements like these.

Writing *and presenting* your best value proposition and capability statement are critical if you are to be effective in selling to this market.

Who can benefit from this book?

- If you are a Minority or Woman Business Enterprise or US Armed Services veteran, this book will help you understand how to present your best business case in the procurement meeting with the people on the other side of the trade show table—that magic matchmaking booth.

- If you are a Supplier Diversity professional or a Council Program Manager, this book can serve as a valuable resource for the suppliers you work with who might need a little extra help with presenting themselves to your company effectively.

- Whether it's for a Council event, a matchmaker, trade fair, or supplier day, this book will help you put your best foot forward. It will help expand your spend, and it will also help your buyers understand some of the challenges that suppliers have in presenting themselves effectively.

First, let's look at some of the challenges ahead...

The Challenge You Face

Corporations are not looking for new suppliers. They just aren't, unless there is a specific need that's been identified in their business. For example, IBM may be looking for manufacturers. Lockheed Martin and Boeing are always hoping to find MWBEs who are in the rarified business of high-end aerospace manufacturing.

For the most part, though, corporations are quite happy with the suppliers they have. In rare cases, there might be a supplier that is underperforming and at risk, but most corporations aren't in the market to usurp perfectly performing suppliers. Changing existing supply channels and partnerships is complicated and expensive. Internal constituencies are resistant to change. As an example, says Dave Nelson, CPM, a top expert in supply chain, 98% of the suppliers that Honda started with in the late eighties still have the business. This makes selling to the Fortune 500 a tough nut to crack.

Well, then, why even bother with supplier diversity? Well, first of all, in some cases, it's the law as it relates to federal contractors. It's also just business best practice. And good PR. Many corporations know that their customers want to buy from companies that do business with women-owned and minority-owned businesses. It's good for the community. It's good marketing. Like gravity, it's a law we can live with.

But if you want a corporation to take you seriously, you'd better darn well be worth the trouble and expense of taking a current supplier out in order to make room for you. So what's your *business* case for asking them to switch? There must be a payoff, a return on investment. Being female, a minority, or a veteran alone just won't cut it. And let me warn you: using that as your door-opener will likely stop the conversation right there.

Corporations are accountable to stockholders. They want to know one thing and one thing only: what are you going to do for *them*? They are not charities, they don't have set-asides, and they aren't offering handouts. While certification programs get you the ticket to play, that is all they do. Once you're certified, it's completely up to you to prove your worthiness and readiness. These corporations are in business to make a profit, and you must show them how your product or service can help them do that. And in order to be considered as a viable supplier, to make a solid first impression, it all starts with some serious research.

Corporations know that there is a good chance that a very smart MWBE or veteran might come up with a product or process that could shave millions off their costs. And that could be *you*. But they're not going to find you unless you approach them in the right way.

Find Your Niche

Even if you sell paper clips, not everyone needs your products. Until you have the resources to really serve everyone, you'll have to choose a market. Whether you choose by industry, by region, or some other criteria makes no difference; you need to choose your sweet spot. If you are a smaller company planning on growing, you may offer several solutions in several different areas of expertise. You'd be wise to choose what you're going to specialize in when it comes to the major leagues, because multitasking doesn't work when you present to the big corporations. What are you *best* at? What do you love doing the most? What are you *known* for? The "what we also do" will shut the door on you when you talk to SD professionals because it muddies the water. A confused mind never buys.

Develop your expertise in one particular area. Get known for what you do best. For example, the areas of IT staffing, general staffing, promotional products and janitorial are jammed, overwhelmed with both women and minority suppliers. In too many cases, they've expanded their services so that they now offer "one-stop shopping." As a result, when they present themselves to SD professionals, they are all, in effect, wearing red suits, wearing red hats, sitting in red boats, sitting in the red ocean waving red flags. No one can see them because they aren't differentiated or unique. That's why they aren't getting business. And neither will you, when you sound like everybody else out on the sales ocean. (For more on this, I recommend you also read *Blue Ocean Strategy: How to Create Uncontested Market Space and Make the Competition Irrelevant,* by W. Chan Kim and Renée Mauborgne.)

How are *you* different? How are *you* already unique? Donovan Casanave is a Supplier Diversity Leader for Shell in Houston. Shortly after he came to work at Shell, he met Angela Starr of Starr Staffing. She was an MBE who had once been homeless, and had built her business up to a $3M company in just a few years. He was mightily impressed. He wanted to give her some business with Shell. So the next day, he went to make his case to Bill, the procurement manager who handles staffing.

"We have to give Angela some business, Bill," says Donovan.

Bill gestured to Donovan to come to his desk, where he sat down and typed in a few strokes on his key board, hit "search," then turned the monitor towards Donovan. On the monitor scrolled a list of 1,500 staffing agencies, 500 of which were highlighted as MBEs.

"When she can differentiate herself from these 1,500 staffing agencies, then we can have a conversation," Bill said.

Both Donovan and Angela share the same problem. She's just like everyone else on the list. She's not unique, she doesn't specialize in any particular skill set that Shell needs; she does "everything." And until she can *own* a particular corner of the oil industry, Shell can't make an argument to use her over any of the other 1,500 companies on their list. She can't make the sale because he can't make the buy.

Don't Paper the Universe

You may have had some success selling your products or services locally. As a result, you're convinced that what you do is a valuable commodity, and that everyone can use it because that's been proven to you by the broad client base you've developed. That may well be true in your hometown. But when you start marketing yourself to the Fortune 500, this approach simply doesn't work. It comes across as scattershot and misguided. You look like you don't have a plan or a market in mind. And this makes it challenging for a sophisticated corporation to do business with you. This barrier will stand until you have clarified that market, developed that niche, and focused your approach on a line of business or market area.

Marcy Davis ran a database management firm in Kansas City. Her firm was struggling, and she was angry and frustrated. Sitting in a supplier-development training in Kansas City, she claimed, "Everyone needs my databases."

When it was suggested that she might consider narrowing that down a little, she repeated, *"Everyone* needs my databases."

The trainer suggested that she might want to look at perhaps hospitals, or government, but she again said, "EVERYONE needs my databases!"

When asked if anyone had approached her to do business, she said, "Well, one…Johnson Controls asked me to get certified nationally if I wanted to do business with them."

"Johnson Controls is a $35 billion company that does a billion dollars' worth of business with minority and women-owned businesses every year. Do you think there might be an opportunity with them?"

Finally it dawned on her. "So you think I should get certified so I can do business with them?" she asked.

Marcy had been so busy trying to sell to people who didn't want or need her databases—and going broke—that a huge opportunity was knocking on her door and she couldn't even see it.

Don't waste your time trying to sell your products to absolutely everybody. You will be exhausted, and you will exhaust your finances trying. Pick out your place in the business community: an industry, a region, an area of expertise—whatever it is—and own it. You will see instant business profits, and credibility to go with it.

Know When to Say When

Susan Gee was determined to get into Apex Corporation, a multi-billion-dollar business that she was sure was a good fit for her. She had been making sales calls ever since she had first met their SD professional, four years ago. More than once she'd been told that she *wasn't* a fit for Apex, but Susan wouldn't take no for an answer. This WBE *knew* that she would eventually wear Apex down. Every year, when she attended WBENC and NMSDC, she visited the Apex booth, and all year long she'd pepper them with literature and phone calls. So much so, that both the local WBENC and NMSDC Councils received complaints from Apex about her aggressive behavior. She received some strong suggestions from the Councils, which repeatedly tried to convince her to back off. But she soldiered on, spending thousands marketing to Apex, who continued to complain while refusing to do business with her.

Finally, Kathy, a program manager at WBENC, asked her bluntly how much she had spent trying to sell to Apex. The number was staggering.

"They don't want you, Susan," Kathy said. "They not only don't want you, but they are talking about you to other companies and poisoning the well there also. It's time to move on and pursue other opportunities."

Susan finally took Kathy's advice, and put her time, money, and resources to work on other accounts.

Sometimes MWBEs and veterans can get focused on one opportunity because they see themselves as a supplier to a PepsiCo or IBM, and they can't let go of that notion. Sometimes you're just not a fit—and nothing that you do is going to change that. Sometimes an RFP has just gone out and you missed the bid, and it's closed for five years. It's no one's fault, it just is. Or maybe you made a bad impression and it ruined your chances, and the door is shut. Accept your losses and move on. The more time and energy you waste on a bad lead, the more resources you take away from other opportunities where you could truly build your business and your reputation. Susan Gee benefited from this advice, and so can you.

Assessing Yourself: A Decision Tree

John Taylor, Manager of Supplier Diversity Development, Global Supply Chain at Delphi Corporation, suggests that MWBEs and veterans periodically have a tough conversation with themselves. Taylor recommends you use this decision tree before, during, and after meetings with major corporations. And, as he puts it, it's best to be brutally honest.

1. Have I done my homework?

   - *Do I know the company's (or division's) core business?*

   - *Do I know and understand their core customers?*

   - *Do I know who my competitors are for the specific business I'm seeking?*

2. How can my company add value—what problem do we solve?

   - *What are my similar success stories?*

3. Am I talking to the right people?

   - *Who have I spoken to?*

   - *Are they the decisions makers?*

   - *Do they have purchasing power and the budget to buy my offering?*

   - *What has been their response to me?*

4. How long have I been targeting this company?

   - *What is the usual timetable for securing this type of business?*

   - *What is the normal cost of acquisition for this type of business?*

   - *Am I outside these norms?*

5. Would the world end if I pursued Tier II (or lower) business?

"So, what do you guys do?"

It was late October. Bill Sanford of Ace Printing walked up to the Lockheed Martin booth clutching his collateral. He'd just gotten his NMSDC certification that year and was a first-timer at the NMSDC conference, so he was eager to do business. He was making the rounds, sure that every big company needed the services of a printing company, and he was ready to provide them. Surely there was enough printing business for his press. It didn't matter what they sold or manufactured, did it? He just wanted their printing business.

He walked up to the representative at the booth and asked, "So, what do you guys do?"

A little taken aback, Bob Thompson explained that Lockheed Martin was one of the largest aerospace contractors in the country. Bill eagerly pressed his collateral into Bob's hands. "Here are some examples of what I can do," he explained. "Can I have your card?" He snatched one from the counter.

"I'll give you a call, and we can talk in a few days!"

Under his breath, Bob muttered, "Not in this lifetime."

Nothing is more annoying to an SD professional than a supplier who wanders up to his or her booth, takes a quick glance at the sign, and asks this inane question. This is a sure way to permanently end all future potential with this company. They will remember you for not having taken the time to find out anything beforehand, and for knowing nothing about a major player in the Fortune 500. There are many companies in the Fortune 500 community whose names are not household words, like AmerisourceBergen (#24) or International Assets Holding (#49, just above Pepsi). If you knew your industry well, you'd know who they were. And therein lies the problem.

One of the chief complaints of SD professionals is that suppliers show up totally unprepared, without having done their research. They haven't registered on the website. They assume their vanilla, one-size-fits-all pitch will work for everyone. This is a sure way to get heaped onto the "no call back" pile. These huge companies have massive websites, chock-full of useful information about their products, their history, lines of service, missions, and goals. They're looking for suppliers whose offerings align with their mission and who can help them achieve those goals. It is not the SD professional's job to educate you on the company while there is a line of six or ten other suppliers waiting to talk to him—that's being rude to the other suppliers, and it's an abuse of the SD professional's time. If there is no crowd, some may be kind enough to give you a company overview or some collateral to read, and others may take mercy on you. But make no mistake: that first impression has been made and will be remembered.

What really impresses an SD professional is someone who has been to the website, who has read industry articles and industry magazines, knows the latest stories on the company, and is familiar with some of the employees in the divisions where they would do work. They know how their product or service would help the company be more successful based on work they've done with similar companies. They speak the industry language but don't necessarily inundate them with "industry speak." This is a surefire way to get their attention.

What's key is that SD professionals come away from that conversation feeling as though you "get them." You "get" the culture, goals, priorities, language, issues, mission—all that's essential to their firm. That's what wins you the opportunity to get to the buyer who means business, and it often means business to you. This is one of the most important things you can do to differentiate. You're the A+ who beats out the thousands of other suppliers who were unwilling to do the homework.

This research demonstrates that you've identified your niche and you know who your market is. You understand your sweet spot, and you know your customer well. You've got a track record, and you can refer to it. If you don't, then you'll have to develop one, and that usually means starting out at a lower Tier to build your credibility. More on this later. At this point, just remember that SD and procurement professionals *always* expect you to do this research. Even if you sell printing.

"I'm an MBE/WBE, and I'm looking for opportunities."

Seven seconds. That's how long it takes to make a first impression. And no second chances. That's about seven words, give or take two. The SD professional has looked you up and down, taken in your appearance, dress, grooming, makeup, hair—everything visual about you—and has made a snap judgment. The next seven seconds will make or break that first impression. This next seven seconds is when you make your *second* impression, and with a BP, Exelon, or Verizon, this could be the biggest seven seconds of your career.

Why on earth would you waste most of those seven seconds restating the obvious? So, what does being an MWBE have to do with this corporation's profitability? How does that impact their ability to do business, get to market, sell to customers? It doesn't. Duh!

Almost as irrelevant is your certification. It's a requirement, but really means very little in the overall scheme of things. It allows you to sell to major corporations, and enables them to count their spend. But that's not the ultimate reason these corporations do business with you. They hire you because of the value you bring, the solutions you offer. They want to hear that right away—in those seven seconds.

Write it down:

What is the problem I solve in my main line of business?

What is the one, best solution that I offer?

How can I bring a company to market more effectively?

If you have a multi-faceted business, you then need to repeat this exercise with *each* product or service you offer. You must be able to answer these questions because that's why they will hire you.

Remember, your certification is like joining the Chamber of Commerce: it is the ticket to play. Business does not come to you automatically just because you are certified. And as you have probably found out by now, registering on corporate websites doesn't get you business either. Networking, selling, and relationship development are what get you business. You can't sit back and wait for the bucks to roll in; you will have a long, lonely wait.

"Just tell me what you want done, and I can do it."

SD professionals who hear this at the trade show booths are tempted to ask the supplier if this includes doing their laundry, sweeping out their houses, and washing their cars. It's a ludicrous statement, yet overeager suppliers, desperate for a chance, say this all the time. It's a sign of immaturity or lack of sophistication in business. Here, the supplier is hoping for a toe in the door somewhere, anywhere, to prove himself or herself. But there is nothing that an SD professional can do with this information; there is nowhere to start. The supplier hasn't done the up-front work to help the SD professional decide on where to use this person in the company.

This kind of statement is an insult to an SD professional's intelligence and to his or her time. At a show, there are often many people, often fully prepared, waiting to talk to them. Here you are, eager and happy and very *un*prepared, taking up this person's time. She doesn't have the bandwidth to teach you how to fit your product or service into the vast offerings of a multi-billion-dollar Fortune 500 corporation, or to find out if you are a better fit at a lower-Tier level. You should know that already. Your enthusiasm notwithstanding, you've just annoyed this SD professional and imposed on her time at the booth. And what you are likely to get is instructions to get registered on the website and keep walking. If this has happened to you a lot, this is why.

Part of your preparation for the show is knowing your niche, and that means narrowing down the number of companies you're going to visit. Out of the four hundred companies on average at WBENC, or the six hundred to eight hundred at NMSDC, you can only see so many booths in a day, perhaps fifteen or so. If you seriously do your research on these companies, you may narrow this down to only seven or eight or even less, but by the time you've done your research, you will have discovered *which* of these huge companies are an IDEAL fit for what you do. And that means that your chances of doing business with them goes up exponentially, and the time spent in those few booths will be time very well spent indeed. A few minutes invested in a few well-chosen booths is far better than a few seconds spent in forty booths in a scattershot approach, with everyone telling you to register on the website and nothing else. Do the math. Another show and no concrete next steps. What would you prefer to take home?

"I can help you meet your supplier diversity goals."

So what? This is one of those lines that makes an SD professional's eyes roll back in her head. What does this have to do with corporate profitability? Nothing.

When you use this as your opening line, you're telling the SD professional that your business isn't very good and that the only *real* value to them is that you think you can help them meet their numbers. What kind of message does that telegraph about your competence, your credibility, your capability? Is that really what you want to say?

SD professionals are serious businesspeople. They are tasked with finding *business solutions* for the company that will (oh, by the way) also help fulfill diversity objectives. Approaching them with this opening line is insulting because it assumes that the only thing they care about is meeting their numbers. They have a huge responsibility to deliver quality suppliers who deliver value for the dollar, who are also (by the way) in the minority, women, veteran and small business space. Their first responsibility is to the business of business, and that means profitability. They may be passionate about the supplier diversity cause, but they must first deliver on the bottom line every single day. They have to be able to justify why the company should take a look at any given supplier. That justification has to be based on whether that new supplier can provide a greater value than an incumbent. And it has to differentiate them from any other new supplier who may have a truly innovative idea. And that's your responsibility, to research and present in a way that the SD professional can immediately understand and embrace. This requires industry knowledge and savvy on your part, not just a knockout opening line.

Advocates

SD professionals are often passionate advocates for minority, women, and veteran suppliers. They believe not only in serving their employers and stockholders, but also in creating opportunities for these constituencies. But once again, corporations are not charities. These businesses must be prepared to do business at this level, or at the lower-Tier level, and *earn the right* to the contracts that are available. Many corporations have mentoring programs, and many go out of their way to help small and emerging companies grow and become thriving enterprises. But they choose the ones that have done their share of research and have demonstrated that they are willing to align themselves with corporate goals and missions, create innovative products and services that will help the corporation succeed, and create a highly symbiotic relationship. In some cases, this has started as a lower-Tier relationship and evolved, which is a very legitimate way to get started in the rarified air of the Fortune 500. You can ask an SD professional for a reference to a lower-Tier contact to help you get underway when you're not a fit for a direct relationship.

Simplicity and Clarity

At the Midwest Council's annual Business Opportunity Fair, an MBE offering IT services was working the booth. He was holding a laminated card that highlighted all of his offerings. It was in small, dense print, and the print was broken up into equally dense boxes, all using industry jargon and "alphabet soup" common to his industry. He stopped to talk at one booth and proudly waved his card at an SD professional.

"This is my capability statement. I'll call you about this in a few days."

He made the rounds to all the booths, and by the end of the show, every single trash can in the show contained at least one of his laminated cards. To a person, the SD professionals said that the card was unreadable, intimidating, overwhelming, reader-unfriendly, and useless.

Your capability statement needs to be simple, straightforward, and memorable, and about fifteen seconds long when delivering it in person to the SD person at the booth.

Your capability statement needs to be built upon an example of a project that you have recently completed or are working on now. It also needs to explain its value or size and the results for your client, and include a reference your prospect can call.

For example:

"We just completed building a $15 million office block for Shell, three weeks ahead of schedule and $2.5 million under budget. You can call John Baker for a reference."

Notice that this is *not* a statement of what you are *capable* of doing, this is something you have *done*. This statement is your résumé of an accomplishment that proves you've done business with the big boys and that you can be taken seriously. More on this later.

Many small businesses get big eyes when they talk to big corporations and say yes to everything. They don't realize that doing so may seal their fate with bankruptcy. Know your limitations. Better to say no to something too big than to take it on and fail completely. Grow slow and be smart.

If you are writing a capability statement for a client, don't throw the kitchen sink onto the page. Use a good graphic designer to put photos, graphics, lots of white space, and quality work into your presentation. Put less information on the page, and use the back to focus on you, your company, and your client testimonials. Focus on just *one* aspect of your portfolio per page instead of trying to cram all that you do on the same page. All it does is confuse and annoy the reader, and just like the laminated card did for the MBE at Midwest, it was a waste of his time and money.

Clarity is power. If someone can't understand or decipher your message, it's lost, and will be thrown away. Don't take that chance on your livelihood.

The Train Wreck

James came at us at speed, blasting into our conversation without apology.

"Where's Brian?" he asked, scanning the room for Brian Tippens, Hewlett Packard's Director of Supplier Diversity.

"He just took a walk down the hall," said Mike McQuarry, SD Manager for HP out of San Ramon. "What can I do for you?"

"My name's James, with BTC Industrial Services. We do janitorial. I want to present what we can do for HP."

"Well, James, an RFP just went out…" Mike started, but James cut him off.

"Oh, an RFP, huh? Well, we can do it all."

I asked, "What makes you different?"

"We're a minority-owned business," said James forcefully.

"That's not a differentiator, and that doesn't impact our profitability," said Mike.

"We do the Air Force base, and we saved them $2 million."

"That may be true, but the RFP went out a few months ago, and it has already been awarded to another company. They now have that concession for the next six years. For the whole country."

"Oh." James left the scene of the crash, unaware of how much damage this train wreck had caused.

What went wrong?

- *James had interrupted a conversation already in progress without an apology.*

- *He hadn't done any background work on HP. If he had, he'd have known about the RFP.*

- *He cut off Mike in mid-sentence.*

- *He said that the differentiator was that they were a minority business.*

In no way did James distinguish himself, other than to impress them as being rude, aggressive, selfish, and interested only in himself and what he had to say. Sure, he's doing business with some big players, but this has made him feel as though he can throw his weight around.

James was working the booths, not working a plan. He was operating out of the assumption that, just because he has some big contracts now, he could force his way into other big companies and get business. It doesn't work that way.

Doing business at this level is a gift and an opportunity. One big contract or even two doesn't give you the right to bully your way into a booth and demand to be attended to. No matter how many contracts you may have, it doesn't earn you the right to be arrogant. Courtesy, regard, respect, and humility will earn you business every single time. If he's serious about getting work with HP and other companies, he needs to be researching their websites, getting in touch with supplier diversity, finding out about the RFPs, and ensuring his company is in on the bids. He needs to have a strategy for who he's going to talk to at each trade show. And above all, he needs to have simple regard for the people in the booths. He has no idea whose conversation he has just so rudely interrupted.

SD professionals are people with feelings and pride and emotions. Like everyone else, they deserve to be treated with respect and courtesy. They have enormously demanding jobs that pull on them in every direction. And they care very much about helping women, minorities, and veterans find opportunities in their companies. The last thing they need is for those very people to abuse their time by being discourteous, but it happens more often than they would care to admit.

It's a Small World

The SD community is a small one, and the members all tend to know one another. In recent years, there have been jobs lost and a few retirements and some movement in the industry, but for the most part, the same players have been there for a while. These people know each other and trust each other's judgment, and want to know when someone can make a solid recommendation on a new supplier, or when an existing supplier has a new offering.

Wherever you start out in the world of supplier diversity, it behooves you to network with regard and courtesy. Where you cannot do business or have no success, leave those relationships warmly and graciously. You don't know if this SD professional will turn up at another company where you might do business in a few years, and the nature of your exchange will be remembered.

SD professionals take great pride in pointing to small companies that they have helped grow into substantial ones. That is what they are all about—helping those companies grow and prosper. They are personally involved with the owners and get to know them and their stories.

When you have done a good job for one of them, word will get around. They like to share a good thing, and referrals will come your way. Keep in mind to under-promise and over-deliver, which is good business strategy for any company. Be patient. In many cases, your opportunity may take a few years to come your way, but when it does, do your absolute best work and be grateful, whatever the size of the project.

This also works in reverse. Delynne Ano, previously Director of Supply Diversity & Sustainability for The Walt Disney Company, talks about how she has, on more than one occasion, gotten far down the road with a WBE supplier—to the point of issuing an RFP—only to have that supplier go on vacation and miss the deadline.

"When we finally reached her, she asked us if we could extend the deadline," Delynne said, sounding exasperated. "Of course we couldn't, and not only that, we took her out of the database.

"In another case—and this goes to prove that we do go into our database for suppliers—we contacted a supplier for her help with sports-related work, and she asked us what ESPN did," Delynne added.

These kinds of mistakes are huge, and they are memorable. They are the kind of *faux pas* that make you unattractive for any future opportunity.

Benefit of the Doubt

When things get tough with a company, remember that it's not always the SD professional's fault. Jan Halstrom recently did $16K worth of consulting work with a multi-billion-dollar company. She was working with the SD professional Jeff Adams, who had taken on additional duties and been promoted. She sent in the invoices, but the company didn't pay them. She continued to bill the company as the months went by, but she still didn't get paid.

Her friends, even her business coach, began to advise her to take action, even legal action. They told her that she was being cheated and that the company wasn't going to pay her. But she believed in Jeff and continued to wait, and send invoices.

Finally, after nine months of dealing with cash flow challenges, Jan finally got paid. The problem had been caused by a different accounting system in the company, and Jeff had done his best to get the invoice paid.

Not long afterward, Jeff moved to another corporation where he plans to utilize Jan in his new capacity. Because she worked with him to keep the relationship healthy, she now has business with this new company. Had she sued Jeff or his company over the $16K, she would have soured her connection and earned a certain reputation in the industry. It's never a good idea to sue, unless you're going to end up with a settlement so big you won't have to work again. Relationships are paramount, and it's always better to try to work things out rather than to bring in the lawyers. It's just not worth it, and not worth ruining your name in such a close community.

"I'm a minority/woman business owner, and you *have* to do business with me."

Nothing, but nothing, shuts the door in your face faster than an entitlement mentality.

"Give a brother a break."

"Just this once."

"Do it for *me*."

The answer is NO. You get work in the Fortune 500 based solely on the merit of your business acumen and the performance of your company.

Diana Diamond runs a speaking company in Colorado. When approached about getting certified as a woman-owned business and taking her diversity training programs to more Fortune 500 companies, she said, "Oh good. They have to pay me additional fees to do business with me as a woman, right?"

This suggestion is a little bit breathtaking in its arrogance. No corporation is going to pay a woman or minority or veteran *extra* just to do business with you. The opposite is true. You have to do *extra* hard work for the right to *earn* the lucrative contracts with these huge corporations. And you have to prove that you've done the research and have the know-how and skill and savvy to help them better serve their customers. And the competition is very, very stiff.

No one owes you anything in this business environment. NMSDC, WBENC, veteran, and other certifications do nothing more than get you a ticket to play. Then the hard work starts, earning your way based on your good products and services. That's what you should be proud of: your ingenuity, your great ideas, your know-how. Corporations want to buy that, and they often have use for those goods and services. It's up to you to help them see where you fit. Don't ruin that opportunity by playing a race, woman, or veteran/disabled card. First of all, it doesn't work. And people will remember how you tried to get in the door. This kind of statement will lead to anger, resentment, and a permanently shut door with any company. Just don't do it. Be above that.

"I'm not leaving until you give me some business."

Laurie Kuecker, SD Manager for American Honda Motor Company in California, recounts the story about an MBE who cornered her at a conference one day. Luis Martinez towered over her, a real physical presence.

He said, "I'm not leaving until you give me some business."

Laurie explained that there wasn't anything she could do for him.

"Well, I'm not leaving until you *do* find me something," he said, leaning into the booth, threateningly.

Laurie felt intimidated but also angry. As an SD professional, she's not responsible for contracts. This isn't part of her job, and she had made this perfectly clear. There wasn't anything she could do for this man. Martinez's physical threat to stay in her face until he got work was all bluff. And, to make it worse, it made her committed to make sure he never got any work with American Honda Motor because he had shown rude and inappropriate business behavior. Martinez was demanding work whether or not there was any place in the company for his skills.

Martinez eventually left. And, of course, Laurie told other SD professionals about him. He ruined his opportunity with a number of companies because of his aggressive approach rather than graciously and respectfully building the relationship based on the value he brought to the company.

It's critical to remember that SD professionals have no contract responsibility. They cannot get you the work unless you are doing supplier diversity training *per se*. Their job is to be the bridge between you and the right contact in the company. But make no mistake—they can and will stop you right at the threshold of the corporation if you step over the boundaries of appropriate behavior and are rude, abusive, or arrogant, or in some other way misuse the right to be in this space. Remember, certification allows you to have access at a very high level, and it is your responsibility to show up with some level of sophistication. These companies owe you nothing. You have to prove to them you're ready to work with them. Again, it's back to your having done your homework. You owe them the courtesy of having figured out how you can be of service.

Your Seven-Second First Impression

Imagine, you're standing in a huge convention hall, surrounded by thousands of other minority and women business owners. Long aisles of booths extend in all directions, and it's noisy. You're standing in front of the International Paper booth facing Debra Voss. You've got six eager people lined up behind you, pushing up against you, waiting their turn to talk to Debra. It all comes down to right here, right now. It's all up to you, these few precious seconds of first impression. She looks at you and asks you, "What do you do?"

What are you going to say?

Supplier Diversity professionals are only interested in one thing: what are you going to do for their company? In many cases, they have arrived at the conference with a clear idea of what the company is looking for and where there are open RFPs or needs. They have a good knowledge of which contracts are set for years to come and where there are current opportunities. And they're committed to finding new help where they can. But first, the help has to serve the corporation's *business* needs.

No matter how good, unique, or special you are, if there are no opportunities, there are no opportunities. In some cases, you may be offering something completely new for which there hasn't been a need before, but that's different. It's up to you to create a need through your value proposition (see the next chapter) and by showing how you can solve a problem or offer a solution through your product or service. But if there is a minority, woman, or veteran incumbent in that role already, chances are very poor that you will pry them out before their contract runs out. You must wait your turn until the bid comes up.

So, let's say you have done your homework and feel you're a good match. You've decided to use humor in your seven seconds. Is this a good idea?

Yes. If you can make someone smile or laugh, you've engaged them at a whole different level. One MBE in Louisiana starts out, "We solve the problem of customer hang-ups." Because this is a double entendre, it usually brings a smile or a laugh, and that buys him more time and interest. The truth is that his product is recordings on hold, the ones you hear on the phone while you're waiting for a person to talk to. This humorous line has gotten him the opportunity to talk to many companies because it's witty and gets the value message across.

Your Value Proposition

That first impression—your value proposition—must be about seven seconds, or seven words long, plus or minus two. It must get across the value you bring to your client. It can rhyme, it can be clever. And, yes, it can be funny, which is a great way to break the ice and get someone to want to hear more. You will need a different value proposition for each unique line of business you offer, one for each different product or service. There is no one-size-fits-all. The purpose of a value proposition is to open the door to giving a ten-to-fifteen second capability statement, which proves that you've got the experience and know-how to do the work you are claiming you can do.

The value proposition is the invitation to listen to more. Keep your audience in mind. That person may already have been listening to pitches for hours. His head may be full of verbiage from other companies. You've got to say something that effectively stops that gerbil cage spinning in his brain that will get a response like, "Wait! This person is different! Pay attention!"

How do you do that?

Start with Research

This bears repeating: before you set foot in the conference, before you sit down at a matchmaker, you must do your research. As obvious as this may be, it's one of the biggest complaints that SD professionals have about suppliers: they don't come prepared. I stress this because so few suppliers do it. You must do your research in advance!

Veronica Manuel, Director, Enterprise Supplier Diversity at Johnson & Johnson, says that many suppliers come to her without any understanding of what J&J does. "They have no idea what kind of business we're in, or what kind of products we make," she explains. "They ask me, 'What do you do? What kinds of things do you buy?' This isn't a good way to approach me."

This *is* a good way to have the door shut in your face. You should already know—*in detail*—what her company does, and you should be telling *her* how you can help J&J be more profitable and more effective as a result of working with you.

These multi-billion-dollar corporations have hundreds of touch points where you can learn about the company. After you've done the research, come with suggestions for where you can get started, where you fit in, where you can make a difference. It's *your* job to *help* the SD professional find where you might fit. The more you can provide this information, and the easier you are to work with, the more support you are going to get. Start with knowledge about what is local to you, for example, with a J&J holding company that might be in your area. Start by showing your knowledge about what is local to you—for example, about a J&J holding company or division in your state. Veronica says that this is often the best way to get started with J&J and work your way up.

Keep the Proposition Sticky and Simple

An MBE freight hauler went to Scott Vowels, President of the Northern California Minority Development Council, and asked for help with his pitch. Scott asked him what he did.

"We do freight."

Scott told the man that he had to come up with something catchier than that, something memorable that the SD professional could keep top of mind.

Three days later, the MBE called Scott back and said, "What about this? YOU CALL, WE HAUL, THAT'S ALL!"

Delighted, Scott said, "Perfect!"

What's so great about this value proposition?

It's short, it rhymes, it's rhythmic, it tends to stick with you while you walk, and it makes you laugh. All very effective ways to make it memorable, and that's what a good value proposition does. All that, and it expresses what this MBE does for a living.

Imagine you're an SD professional. You have thousands of suppliers plying you with their sales pitches at NMSDC. You try to remember what they said, to decipher the notes you wrote on their cards. You also have to try to remember something of what each of them had to say while you're then taking those messages—thousands of them—to your internal customers: IT, Marketing, Transportation, HR, Purchasing, Engineering, the CEO—whoever might be the end user for your goods and services. What chance do you have if your message is long and complex?

Think of this another way. There's a game many of us played in grade school. All the kids would form a circle, and the teacher would tell the first child a secret, which that child would then whisper to the next child, and so the secret would pass from child to child until it got to the end of the circle. That last child would reveal his or her version of the secret, now convoluted and altered, and everyone would laugh. That's a funny game, unless it's your very important marketing message.

Your value proposition opens the door and identifies you as unique. It is what sets you apart. Like those slogans, "Got Milk?" and "Just Do It," value propositions identify organizations and brands in such a way as to set them aside from the rest.

Your value proposition is designed to get the SD to respond with:

"Tell me more."

"I'm interested."

"Explain what you mean."

"Okay, go on," or some other signal that you've got the green light to keep talking.

If you sound like, look like, feel like, talk like, and present like everyone else in your field, you will likely get the cold shoulder. Go to the portal, sign up, wait and hope.

To be more creative, use your thesaurus. Write creatively. Don't use the same adjectives and verbs your industry always uses. Go to your customers and ask them to describe the job you've done for them. Use their descriptors.

Better yet, fill in this sentence: I/We are the *only* one(s) who_____.

Know how you are unique!

Remember, if you are in janitorial, IT, staffing, or promotional products, you have a huge challenge ahead of you to find a niche and be able to differentiate yourself. The more general you are in your services, the less attractive you will be. Find a way to fill a void in the market. It's your job to make yourself an attractive partner to these companies. What are they missing? Do your research. What is the biggest problem or complaint they have about your industry? What have you done differently to respond to that problem?

A janitorial service recently decided to differentiate themselves by highlighting their high level of supervision and low employee turnover, both rare in the industry, and to help focus on why they get such high ratings from their customers.

How are you unique?

Value Proposition Examples

So what does a value proposition sound like?

"I teach charisma." (motivational speaker)

"I get people out of hot water." (lawyer)

"We build dream buildings." (construction)

"We translate the untranslatable." (translation services)

"We craft future possibilities." (financial services)

Any of these could be a value proposition.

Or you can work from another model: how you solve a problem.

"I solve the problem of unprepared suppliers." (supplier diversity training)

"We solve the problem of uncollected receivables." (collection services)

"I solve the problem of employee turnover." (HR services)

"We solve the problem of wandering eyes." (optometry services)

This last one is funny because it can be taken two ways. That's one of the best kinds of value proposition: the double entendre, where you can have some fun with its interpretation.

The problem-solving version is great because corporations all have problems in every aspect of their business. If you're smart enough to figure out where they are, especially in the green space, then you can offer solutions to those problems. Sustainability is one area that is increasingly attractive, and companies are definitely looking for solutions. Where can you help? Can you offer a green solution in what you are doing, and can that be what differentiates you from the competition? That may cost you a bit in the beginning, but it may well be the one thing that determines who gets that multi-million-dollar contract.

If you are in IT solutions, your challenge is to find a particular industry that you can serve, instead of trying to be all things to all people, and then continue to add services to your lineup. As more and more corporations are bringing IT inside, you may have to offer yourself as a subcontractor. And in many cases, you may have to start locally. It strikes SD professionals, especially the large international firms, as ludicrous when a boutique IT services house approaches them and wants to be their provider. This shows a real lack of sophistication on the supplier's part, a dearth of research, and fundamental misunderstanding of how things work at this level. Understand who you are and where you can fit, and understand your capacity.

What will distinguish you from everyone else is when you can use a client's language, data, and statistics with him—a company can't argue with its own data. Then, when you can use that information compellingly and demonstrate how, with your product or service, you can solve a problem, you are well on your way to getting an appointment.

A Word on Multiple Value Propositions

Most times, you're going to have multiple value propositions based on the different lines of business and products that you offer. There is no one-size-fits-all. Most businesses have a variety of offerings, so you're going to need to develop a statement for each unique offering you have.

But, each time you approach a corporation, you should only present *what fits that company*—not everything you offer—and it needs to be based on the research you've done in advance. So you tailor your approach and present only what is appropriate, instead of throwing everything in your toolkit at the SD professional and hope that something sticks.

Writing Your Value Proposition

Where do your ideas for a value proposition come from?

They come from your experience with customers, what your clients say, and the value that you bring.

To get new ideas for a value proposition, interview your best clients. What do they tell you? What do they say about you, and what words do they use to describe you and your business?

It's important to be careful NOT to use terms that everyone else is using to describe your services. When you say that you provide great service, save clients money, or give service with a smile, you sound just like everyone else. You're in the business of standing out. Why did your clients choose you over your competition? Why are they loyal to you?

Choose Your Words with Care

Words can be so powerful. Those first few seconds of first impression are lasting, so those first few words must be well-chosen and commanding, and convey a clear image of the work you do. Then the door opens for them to hear your capability statement, your quick résumé.

In writing your value proposition, avoid "I/we help companies..." This is a weak statement-starter when you are talking business, and you can do much better. Use powerful words like build, create, transform, develop, drive. Find colorful words that create a picture in listeners' minds—forge, unearth, transfigure—so that they can imagine you doing this work for their company and making the same difference.

Here's another way to think about it. Imagine your client is driving along the freeway, and your value proposition is a line of text on a billboard. Would they take action? Would they even notice?

Start by writing five rough-draft value propositions for your top offerings. Write and rewrite these value propositions, and then practice them. Shorten them again and again and again, until they are crisp and clean and to the point. What's key is to practice them with someone who isn't familiar with your business so that you can get appropriate feedback on whether the impact of your opening statement is understood.

Here is an example of a first draft for your value proposition:

"We are a painting company. We've been in business for forty-five years. We do your walls, your décor, everything. We help you make a better first impression for your clients. We're a minority-owned business so we can help you make your numbers."

Now here's the second version of that value proposition:

"We help you make a better first impression to your clients by changing your colors."

And the short version:

"We improve the color of your bottom line."

This final version is swift, gets across an intriguing idea that invites a question: "What do you mean by that? Tell me more." The whole idea here is to trim, trim, and trim some more. You can always fill in more information later. Now is the time to intrigue, tickle their fancy. Get the idea?

Jerry Seinfeld, the comedian, says that it takes him at least an hour to remove three words from an eight-word sentence to make it funnier. That's good writing. And it will take you at least that kind of commitment to shorten your value proposition to make it less wordy.

Again, while you may think it's important to tell the SD professional or procurement person your company's whole story, this is not the time or place. Keep that billboard in mind. You only have seconds! And it's not about cramming those seconds full of information. It's about getting essential information into a few seconds in such a way that the person you're addressing is intrigued, engaged, and inspired to ask you for more information. They hear something in your offering that stands out. Out of all the people they've heard that day, this is new, sharp, funny, or somehow worth taking a moment to hear out. That's the purpose of your value proposition— nothing more, nothing less. And it's up to you to edit, edit, edit—get that opening statement down to the bare minimum so that there's less to digest but enough to make someone say yes to you.

Remember, those now well-known catchphrases "Got Milk?" and "Just Do It" took many months of writing, study, work, and miscues. Your value propositions won't happen overnight.

What to Cut from Your Value Proposition

What's not relevant right up front?

> *Your minority, woman, or veteran status.*
>
> *Your client list (at least, not yet).*
>
> *Your years in business.* (This detail may be relevant at a later point, because so many new businesses fail within the first five years. But talk about this after you have expressed your value proposition.)
>
> *Where your business is located.* (This is relevant if you are in a HubZone, but again is only important much later in the conversation. It doesn't impact the company's profitability.)

Your opening statement should cut to the chase:

> *. . .for this particular company, for this particular industry, for their particular need:*
>
> *What is the problem you solve?*
>
> *What is the solution you offer?*

How can you express this by using their industry terms? Their language? This could be very powerful for you if you have a background or experience in the industry. You can also learn the language by studying the website, reading industry publications, and interviewing people in the industry.

More Examples

Some additional examples of value propositions:

First draft: "I am an optometrist. I have thirty years in the business. I can work with all insurance programs. I'd like to be considered as a provider to your programs at XYZ corporation."

Final: "I solve the problem of wandering eyes."

This value proposition works because it's a pun. It's going to make someone laugh at first, which is perfect. The original draft stated the obvious (to be considered as a provider) and gives information that is better discussed later. The final version breaks the ice, is witty and different. This vendor doesn't sound like everyone else who walked up.

First draft: "We are a woman-owned company that has been in business for 27 years. We have twelve employees. We are in four states in the Midwest, based in Chicago. We help you get the dollars that are owed you by your outstanding accounts. We guarantee our results."

Final draft: "We solve the problem of uncollected receivables."

The first version has much information that has nothing to do with profitability. By getting rid of it and concentrating on the value she brings, the second version gets to the heart of what her company can do for the client.

First draft: "I do personal training sessions for executives in major corporations. I work with people who have weight problems, people with high risk factors for health, who travel a lot, or who otherwise just want to be in better health. I have all the proper certifications and have a broad background in the field."

Final: "I solve the problem of the last belt hole."

Again, here there is some intrigue: what does he mean by this? There's a mystery to be solved. The first version is extremely wordy and takes a lot of time to say. The final version invites a visual, a smile, and a question or two. And gets his foot in the door. Not too many execs *don't* have a problem with that last belt hole, and this approach nails it.

Your Capability Statement

If your value proposition opens the door, then your capability statement is the sales pitch the door opens to reveal. This is your postcard of proof. This is where you give an example of work that you are doing for a similar company, results that they enjoyed, and a reference. In a nutshell, about ten to fifteen seconds. In moments, they know you're a player.

So to recap, you're not telling them what you *can* do, but what you *have done*. This is key. This could also be about a project that is in play right now, but it has to be recent, within the last year or so.

Examples:

"We designed a $15 million green casino for Harrah's, came in $3 million under budget and four weeks ahead of schedule. You can ask Bill Schoenfeld for a reference."

"I conducted a series of sales seminars for Microsoft Corporation this past fall. It was an $80,000 project, and it resulted in a 35% increase in fourth quarter sales. You can ask Susan Richter for a reference."

"Last winter we designed, organized, and managed a $500K gala event for AT&T at the Las Vegas Hilton. It was their most well-attended sales event, and Ann Riley says that it was their most successful yet. You can call her for a reference."

What have you done that has proven you can make a difference? What work have you done for a similar industry that shows you can work at this level? What proves you can *scale up* to the Fortune 500?

Here is where you want to mention any strategic alliances that you have that allow you to take on national and international work. And if you don't have any now, it's time to find them. Know whether you can supply what's necessary to do the job and, if you can't, bring a bigger gun to the table. That shows your savvy. No one gets to the top alone, and if you're struggling, it's time to partner. It's a wise supplier who can let go of their logo and throw in with another company to go after the multi-million-dollar contracts—and create the jobs that go with them. Your capability statement proves that you have the experience, knowledge, and capacity to play at these higher levels.

Say something like this:

"We are a two-man operation, but we have a strategic alliance with Astridge Corporation, which has operations in twenty-nine states. They are also a minority-owned company, and this gives us the ability to provide the coverage and services to our clients."

Again, you want the SD professional to come away from this interaction with you saying, "She (or he) *gets* us." That means you speak their language, you understand the culture, you have been around the website. You've read the articles, you know the industry, you are sophisticated enough to know what part of the company you belong in. All of this makes their job so much easier. And it makes them want to help you much more.

Sure, there are times when the SD professional will help out a total newcomer, help you find your way around the company, and get you started. But they cannot do this—will not do this—for everyone. If they feel you have a product that has a chance, you might get some extra assistance. But, guaranteed, if you walk in with an arrogant attitude of "it's all about me," then you're not going to get anything but an invitation to go to the back of the line.

If you want to be taken seriously at the Fortune 500 level, you can't look, feel, or act like a rank beginner. You need to do your research and understand how the game is played. And that means understanding where you fit in and how you can make an impact. That is *your* job, not the SD professional's job, and the harder you work to find where you fit, the faster you will get in the door if there is a fit for your product or services.

Developing Your Capability Statement

It's important to have a bank of examples of completed projects clearly in mind when talking to prospects. This will give you legitimacy and also build your confidence. You'll use these examples not just when you're standing at a booth, but also when you're in conversations at receptions and events where people want to know about what you do and what you have accomplished. It's key to be able to call up quick examples of your achievements from top of mind based on who is standing next to you, be it Bausch & Lomb or National Grid. Being prepared to mention these work examples will keep you from being tongue-tied, and you can present your company's capabilities effectively and appropriately.

Go back through your business for this past year or so. Look at what you've achieved, the big contracts you've done, the work you've accomplished. What are you proud of? Which have been your biggest wins?

Write up your capability statement based on this model:

- *When did it happen? (make it recent—within the year, if possible)*
- *Who was it for? (preferably in a similar industry or vertical)*
- *What was the size or scope of the project? (a specific number, like $100K or $25M)*
- *How did you improve the business? (25% increase in profits, sales, etc.)*
- *Who is a reference they could check with?*

For example:

"We did a $600,000 training project for McDonald's mid-level managers throughout the Midwest in 2009, and got a 20% increase in productivity by the end of 2010. You can call Alan Shepherd, Director of Development, for details."

"By using our product, Apex's fleet was able to improve gas mileage by 18%, saving them $6 million. You can check with Ted Suarez in Operations."

"Our new LED technology lights improved energy efficiency at Severn's plants by more than 12%. This resulted in a total of $12 million in annual savings. You can call Steve Baker for a reference."

"We translated the Office Depot website into Spanish and that has made their sales skyrocket by 300% in the Spanish community. Since then, our translation services have been utilized throughout the rest of the company in all aspects of their international business, to help them close deals and do more business overseas. You can ask Alina Braunsteen for a reference."

"We outfitted three of ABC's plants with uniforms at a cost of $59K, saving them more than 30% with our green products and manufacturing processes. We have been asked to outfit four more plants next year, another 1,200 employees, a $120K project for us. You can call Kaleem Mohammad for a reference."

If You're Brand New

Dream big, but start small. Not everyone who wants to do business is going to have a track record and can draw from their experience with a similar company. But you will have your experience that led you to start out. Let's say you worked for Caterpillar for twenty years, and now you're selling consulting services on your own and you want to sell to large companies like Caterpillar. You can use your experience and background to validate your know-how. Don't sell yourself short, but be clear in your own mind about what your capabilities are. How big can you go? What is your capacity?

Large corporations want to know if you can handle their massive requirements. If you're a home-based business making candles, and you've got dreams of selling to Walmart and making millions, are you ready for that amount of business? One order from Walmart could bankrupt you, and this is where understanding scale is so critical. Best to start small and work up, until you have an understanding of how big BIG really is when you're dealing with multi-billion-dollar companies and massive inventories. Here is where it just makes good sense to work with a strategic partner who can teach you the ropes, show you how to grow, and mentor you (see the next chapter). Large corporations also have mentoring programs, so inquire whether such a program is available.

Know when to say no. Many small companies have gone out of business or been damaged by saying yes to big contracts because their eyes got bigger than their capacity to deliver. Doing business with big companies is very exciting for the ego. But when you're in contract negotiations, beware of promising, "Yes, we can do that," or "Sure, no problem," or simply saying yes to everything they ask of you. Before you know it, you've signed on to a whole list of responsibilities you later find you can't live up to. You then show up hat-in-hand, all apologies. Better to bite off smaller pieces and do an amazing job. Grow your company more slowly through well-placed opportunities that are your core competency. This measured pace allows the corporation to learn to trust you and your good judgment over time, and that protects both of you. These big corporations make promises to their customers based on being able to trust their suppliers—you—and that means you have to be able to live up to your promises.

Creating Collaborations

Chicago, 2009, the Chicago Business Opportunity Fair check-in line, about 8:30 a.m. Fumbling around putting on my badge, I bumped into Haven Cockerham, CEO of the MBE HR firm Cockerham & Associates. We exchanged hellos and found out that we were in similar businesses, and we exchanged cards, saying that there may eventually be a time that we might work together. We parted ways, and I thought, "Nice guy. You never know."

By the end of the day, I was scrambling to find Haven's card. Archer Daniels Midland had asked me to help them with a project that I could not do without Haven's expert help. It required his broader expertise, and I needed him as a strategic partner. The next time I saw Haven was at breakfast in Decatur, Illinois, in preparation for our first meeting with ADM and the beginning of what has become a very good partnership. Because Haven has people all over the country, and is a more sophisticated company in the HR space, I can bring him in to my biggest corporate meetings as my "gorilla in the room." In many cases, I am able to score a phone call to get us both on a first-time conference call to begin a potential contract conversation with a new client, which opens up brand new business for us both. This is where we serve each other. At no time do I worry about Haven taking my business away, nor would he have that concern about me. This is an excellent working relationship and is a perfect example of how a one-person firm can work with a much larger, diverse firm to create opportunities.

Who might you work with who could help you get opportunities, help you open doors? Whose business can you help? How can you as a smaller, more nimble, and diverse business bring a solution to a larger Prime corporation doing business with a Fortune 500 company?

If you're a $100K, $200K, or even $500K company, in most cases you're not going to be First Tier or Prime to most major corporations. You'll need to research which companies are doing business directly with these corporations, and market yourself to the Primes or to those companies doing business with the Primes. In some cases, the SD professionals will give you the names of the companies where you might be a fit. Not always. If you know your industry, you should already know the players and where you can partner. Whether you are a Tier Five or a Tier Two makes no difference. The point is that the money is still green, and it gives you the opportunity to develop and grow your business and your reputation over time. There are many Tier Threes that are now Primes because they waited their turn.

This May Not Be Your Market

It's easy to get excited about doing business with companies that are household names. It's impressive to be able to say that you sell to GM or Ford, to Kraft or Coca Cola. But sometimes this just isn't the right market for you. It might be that your real sweet spot is a market that is actually several levels down and a perfect fit. And what's happening is that you're trying so hard to sell out of your league that you're losing the real opportunity—where your niche really is—because of the stars in your eyes about the big names.

Every company needs that niche market, but here we're addressing size. You can make a great deal of money and a whole lot of profit selling to multi-million-dollar companies as opposed to multi-*billion*-dollar companies. Many companies do very well in their own localities and their own regions, without ever selling to the Fortune 500. But if you believe this is your market, and you have been realistic about your size, your capability, and what you're ready to deliver and what you can reasonably do in the marketplace, then more power to you. Either way, remember the basic rules: start in the company's divisions and work up. As you grow, you can acquire; as you acquire, you gain size and capacity; as you gain capacity, the bigger corporations will look at you as a higher-level supplier. Or, as we said earlier, find that strategic partner who can give you both access and experience.

Strategic Networking

Finding a collaborative partner means getting out of the office and connecting. Seventy-five percent of the American public is uncomfortable with networking, mostly because we're afraid of rejection. But this is about your business, and it's about creating opportunities. The ability to create collaborative connections with others is one of the most important skills of the twenty-first century. This is no time to be a wallflower!

First, recognize that networking isn't about you; it's about helping others feel at ease around you. It's about making them feel comfortable, as though the space around you is your living room and they are honored guests. Let them relax in your presence as you ask questions and help them feel like they're welcome. It's not your job to be entertaining. It is your job to find out as much as you can to see if you have commonalities. That's what you're there to do: find potential partners, see if your values align, and see how your companies might work together.

Network in Your NAICS Code

In your search for a collaborative partner, find companies that do what you do—but not exactly. Where are your weaknesses? Seek out competitors who are good where you are not, and create alliances where you can do work together. Ironically, your competition is the source of some of your best partnership potential. Look for companies and individuals who can bring value to your offerings and who can build your company's reputation. Look especially for larger companies that could use your particular expertise, your unique product or service or solution. Bring a service-first attitude, along with a lawyer and an accountant, when it comes time to do the paperwork. An old-fashioned handshake isn't enough when it's time to split the profits. Make sure your paper trail is solid and that you are taken care of properly.

Ann Sullivan runs an IT staffing firm. She complains that when she has tried to work with a particular Prime in the past, she has been faced with cherry-picking on their part—and very limited profits for her company. Her challenge is that she needs to not take deals that aren't good for her company and her people in the first place, and be smart enough to walk away from them. In a shrinking market this may be difficult, but when it's damaging to the firm and demoralizing to her, it's just not worth it. This is true for any business, whether it's IT staffing or any subcontracting deal. Know what you are signing, know what you are giving away, understand the consequences of putting your name on the line. This is good advice in *any* case, but when it's all about developing partnerships, it's truly key. Be enthusiastic and smile, and have your lawyer handy. As Ronald Reagan said, "Trust, but verify."

Check the Community

When looking for a partner, you'll find all sorts of resources throughout the community: your local NMSDC Council, WBENC organization, Chamber of Commerce, diverse chambers, churches, and business associations. The professional associations you have joined (or should join if you haven't yet) provide many opportunities to meet your peers and people affiliated with your industry. Look around. The more you research, the more ways you will see that you can bring someone into your work to create new business for your target market or a new way to present your product or service. It takes a little ingenuity, but ingenuity is what made you an entrepreneur!

Get very active in all these organizations. Take on leadership positions and get known as a leader. Take a stand on issues. Get connected with other leaders. Go to conferences and find out who are the best practitioners in your industry. That's where you're going to want to create your partnerships. And if you've done a good job of creating an excellent reputation for yourself and your business, they will be interested in working with you, too. Approach them with a value proposition for working together just as you would approach a Fortune 500 company for business: what's the benefit to them of working with you as a partner? How do they gain? How do you both make money, gain market share? If you've done your research in advance, this should be a clear proposal. After all, they'd be taking a chance on you, too.

A Word on Networking

Summer, Los Angeles, the California Black Chamber of Commerce Awards gala. I was standing in line with two SD professionals I'd just met from Sun Energy, Terry and Ann. We were waiting to be assigned our table for the evening festivities.

Larry Landers, an MBE who owns an office supply firm, moved up the line to join us. He recognized me from the supplier diversity program I'd done that morning. He smiled at us, then immediately launched into a tirade about Office Depot.

"Those b - - - - - ds! They came into this town and took all my business! I can't believe what they did!" he said at volume, his face distorted in anger. Terry and Ann took three steps back. Larry continued his rant, "I went to all my clients and told them 'I *made* you, I gave you good prices so that you could grow! YOU OWE ME!"

The three of us had stepped back to give him plenty of room, and, noticing this, Larry turned from us and went back to his previous place in line in a huff.

Ann leaned towards me and whispered, "We're not going to be doing any business with *him,* are we?"

Larry made two choices. First, he chose not to approach Office Depot to become a Tier Two provider. Second, he chose to attack his previous clients, which certainly must have at least disappointed, if not antagonized, many of them, making him lose more business. Third, he had too much to drink at the reception and went ballistic in front of other potential clients—specifically, ruining his potential business with Sun Energy, who will likely also talk about him to other SD professionals.

Larry may have reasons to be frustrated, but he needs to remember that he is always in the public eye. When people are dressed for a gala, the name tags are gone and no one knows who's who without an introduction. It pays to be very circumspect. And above all, it pays to know your alcohol limit. Never, ever take the chance that you will embarrass yourself as Larry did. Know if you have an issue with alcohol and take appropriate steps. Recognize that if you have a limit of two, only drink one. Business and alcohol don't mix well, even among friends. Where there are potential clients, you absolutely must be on your best behavior, and in control.

You're On, 24/7

Networking is so much more than an event where you put on your "hat" and go shmooze. These days with the advent of electronics in every aspect of our lives we are nearly completely transparent. We are available to each other 24/7. Every conversation, every hand-shake, every phone call, email, text, or tweet is part of our legacy.

Have you ever had a bad day, gotten an annoying email, and fired off a livid response? Then regretted it a few moments later? How many times has the immediacy of technology worked to our disadvantage when a cooler head should have prevailed? It's so easy to type first, hit "Send," and worry about it later. It's rather like the Wild, Wild West of iPhones, only now we're shooting words.

Your Internet presence is all part of your persona and can affect how you're perceived as a business owner, professional, or supplier. You are in the spotlight at all times. And like Larry in our previous story, you never know who's in your immediate vicinity at any given time. No matter where you are, you're responsible for your behavior and how you're impacting others. What you say about your clients, your competitors, anyone, reflects on you. What kind of legacy are you leaving at the conferences you attend? How are you being re-membered? How are you showing up after hours? Are you more memorable there than at the booths?

Which brings up one more item about today's social media. If you use Facebook, LinkedIn, Twitter, or any of the many other sites, remember that your clients do as well. Do not put up inappropri-ate material on these sites—material that could embarrass you, be misinterpreted, or otherwise put you or your company in a poor light. This is part of networking, too. Photos of you drunk at a beach party, in states of undress, or in other conditions less than dignified can cost you opportunities. This is the world we live in today, so manage your impressions.

But, remember also, when you are connecting with SD professionals and corporate execs at NMSDC, WBENC, and Council events, to turn your sales pitch OFF. It's time to relax. That old saw about how people do business with people they like is still repeated often because it happens to be absolutely true. So be yourself, be authentic, be comfortable in your own skin. Find out about people's lives, families, backgrounds, likes, dislikes—who they are when they're not working the booths and answering the phones. Not only will they appreciate your personal interest, you will make some lovely friends along the way. Stop seeing every corporate exec as a goal to be accomplished and see them as the person they are. This will shift the dynamic and allow you to have a real exchange that is easy and comfortable. The next time you connect, it will be as friends. It will be easier to connect by phone, and your emails will be answered faster. The business will come when it comes. Start enjoying the people and the journey along the way, and you will be amazed at how rich the experience becomes.

Don't Be Addicted to Your Logo

Speaking about managing our impressions, we love our logos. So many small businesses get started, spend a lot of money developing a shiny new logo, and then take all kinds of classes on branding. That's great. But many, many American businesses are around that $100K mark in revenue, and they won't grow without a joint venture or a buyout by another large company. While it's understandable that you're proud of your baby, the real opportunities are in partnerships and collaboration. And, as I've said, that's the only way most small companies are going to get in the door of these huge corporations. That means letting go of that logo, and being willing to play nice to get bigger contracts.

The only way America will grow is if her diverse and women's businesses grow, as those are the engines that will run America's economy over the next many decades. America has lost sixteen million Fortune 500 jobs over the last ten years. In all frankness, $100K a year isn't big enough to hire people and keep the economy running at a healthy pace. Small businesses need to grow to $500K and then to well over $1M to really be impactful in the American economy, and that means collaborating and getting serious about sales, marketing, and knowing how to run your business.

Business School Programs

Learning how to run your business is a whole different book. But SD professionals can often be of real help, as can Councils and WBENC, and you can find help to get better at managing and running your company. There are a number of great business schools around the country. Two programs stand out as schools that suppliers can attend through scholarships or on their own: Tuck Dartmouth School of Business and Kellogg School of Management. These programs challenge the business owner with a complete immersion and a week away from the day-to-day operations. It's a rare opportunity to plan, envision, and create your company from a global perspective.

You will learn financial, managerial, operational, and strategic planning skills and much more. These programs take advantage of your time away from the details of the business to give you the chance to imagine. You will come back to your business with a plan of action, refreshed, and ready to take on the world.

These programs have different qualifications for participation. No matter which program you decide to enroll in (Tuck has two levels and you can do both), it will be well worth your time. Alumni members talk not only about the quality of the program but the lifelong business connections they made during their time away. You gain personally and professionally. Find out more at your local Council or WBENC office, or pay your own way. You'll be very glad you did.

Charrisse Brown took the advanced Tuck course in late 2009. She found herself immersed in financials, not her strong point. While she struggled through the numbers, she made sense of the program and came away with a powerful commitment to her company and a list of eleven major goals. Back at her office, she put the list away and didn't look at it again until three months later.

At that point, she'd already achieved four of the major goals, including starting to write a book. She also had begun to turn her business around and was opening up a new line of business to her clients. In another seven months, she had completed nine of her goals, including finishing her book and doubling her sales for the new year, completely turning her struggling business around. She credits Tuck with transforming her business, teaching her financial skills, and setting her on track to writing two more books. She's also learned to give herself the occasional vacation to envision the future for her company.

It Takes Time

Developing business with huge corporations takes time—sometimes many years. During the course of developing a relationship with a big company, your contact may get promoted, leave the company, or take a new job. In 2010, those of us who loved working with Tanya Allen Easter were sad to see her move into commodities at Chevron, but we were pleased for her personal achievements. We then turned to Ron Rodrigues, her replacement, to develop the new relationship as he took the reins in supplier diversity. And so it is in the corporate world. People move, and you must be able to adapt. That means networking with others in the department, and being willing to immediately connect with new arrivals when change happens.

The other truth about the time element is that big corporations simply move slowly. It takes time and a lot of money to move an incumbent supplier out. If you're the one being considered, this isn't likely to happen overnight unless there's an emergency and you've already been highly recommended by a trusted source. Even that is very rare. Expect to be carefully vetted, tested, and put under a microscope. Expect to meet a lot of people and have plenty of meetings. Expect paperwork, RFPs, long waits, and having your patience tried. Whatever you do, don't get into your SD professional's face and demand action.

One MBE I know in Louisiana is in the drilling business, and every time I see him he's frustrated. But, also, every time I see him, he's made significant progress with the top oil companies in the country. The last time we spoke, he said, "Shell had me in to meet with their top engineers. Do you think that's something?" I said it was indeed something and that he was a lot further along than the year before, when he had not even gotten his foot in the door. He simply has to work through the labyrinth of processes that the company uses to make their decision, and he will have his contracts.

John Ballard works for a Tier One company that vets MWBEs for Shell. He met with, and was impressed by, the CEO of a WBE freight company in Louisiana, Sheila Simpson of Carryall Freight. He told her she was being considered for a contract with Shell and that she would be hearing from him.

Over the next few days, Sheila started calling. Not once, not twice, but *five times a day.* At first, her tone was polite.

"John, this is Sheila. I'm very excited about the contract we talked about. Please call me when you have word. Thanks!"

John didn't call her back because, of course, he had nothing to tell her. This process was going to take many months.

Unfortunately, Sheila kept calling, and her tone got shrill. By the end of the third day, she became demanding.

"John, you promised me you'd get back to me. I thought we had a deal. I understood that you were going to get back with me. Please call me right away. This is Sheila from Carryall Freight."

By the fourth day, Sheila was threatening John with legal action!

"John, this is breach of contract! You promised me business, and you haven't gotten back to me in four days! What's going on here? I demand that you call me right away!"

At this point, John called Sheila and explained in no uncertain terms that not only was there no business yet, but she was only one of a number of businesses being considered. He had made no such commitment to her and said that this was a process that typically takes *at least* six months. She was overly eager and simply didn't understand. He was patient with her, though, and understood that this was her first time working with such a large company.

Sheila was lucky that John was willing to see her lack of sophistication and work with her. In most circumstances, her actions would have been enough to remove her not only from the vendor list for that opportunity but also from all future opportunities.

Do your due diligence. Find out what the process is, especially if you are just starting out. Find out the timeline and settle in for the long haul. It will be worth it. Your graciousness, courtesy, and kindness will get you much more business than being grasping, demanding, and impatient.

A good case in point: since 2004 I've been trying to get business with Southern California Edison (SCE), a huge utility company. I've met Dennis Thurston and other members of the SCE team at conferences all over the country. Dennis has always shown interest, and we've talked, and I've been referred to other members of the team as well. Every year, I've kept up my contacts with various members of the SCE team, sent emails, and continued my sales pitches. Nothing happened. But I never gave up. And I didn't get frustrated. In 2010, six years later, I finally had the opportunity to do my first program for the company. SCE hired me to do a supplier forum—*and* a series of training programs for them during the summer—and now we are planning to do more work together. I am expanding my relationship to other areas within the company as they get to know my skills and like what I do for them. They are turning out to be one of my top clients. By being patient, by staying in touch respectfully and keeping them apprised of new programs, products, and skills I'd developed, something finally evolved. And now the door is wide open.

It can take from eighteen months to six years for you to create a contract with a huge corporation. When it's time, it's time, not a moment sooner or later. You cannot force it. And above all, calling and complaining to the SD professional about how you're not getting treated fairly isn't going to make you popular. They don't control the contracts.

Know the SD Ropes

Keep in mind that it's up to you to market yourself. Supplier diversity is just one way into the company. Along with marketing, you must also network, publish, develop your website—do all those things that a business does to make itself known. Sometimes business comes to you that doesn't come through the SD door. If this happens, be sure that you communicate this to your SD professional so that they can count your spend. This is critical, and it builds your relationship with that office.

If a division or company within the corporation wants to do business with you without using your certification, don't cooperate. Communicate this to your SD professional and let them handle the situation. The corporation wants to count the spend, and they also want you to get your contract. Most corporations with a commitment to supplier diversity have strong policies in place, and it's rare to find people who don't support them. However, it does happen.

Another consideration is that SD professionals differ in whether they prefer for you to work solely through them or to work the company on your own and just get back to them. Whatever they ask, honor their request. Let's say they ask you not to go around them, and they say there are no contracts for you at this time. You go over their head to find a program manager, who immediately complains to the SD professional that you're harassing them about business. You will probably never work in that company. And you'll be blacklisted elsewhere. When it's no, it's NO. There are how many companies in the Fortune 500? Let it go, be respectful, and move on.

On the other hand, SD professionals may be perfectly happy for you to work the system and get back to them with your successes. Just be sure you do, so they can count the spend. They're giving you free rein. Respect this freedom and report your contracts to them. It's simple courtesy and good business.

I recently had a situation where an outside consultant gave me a lead about potential business at a major utility, where I also know the supplier diversity director, Susan. I could have followed up on the lead directly based on the consultant's information, but instead I ran the information by Susan. Good thing I did. The information wasn't entirely accurate. Had I approached this contact with misinformation and bad assumptions, it would have been embarrassing, and it would also have put Susan in an awkward position as she is trying to help me get business at this utility. I believe that it's important to let your SD professionals be your champions internally, and let them work the system for you. This builds trust and a good working partnership, and that's how good business gets done.

This system is in place to work for you to get business and, when you work the system, it does pay off. When you abuse it, you pay a big price in lost relationships and your good reputation, the heart and soul of your business.

Spread It Around

If you get a chance to do a lot of work with a major corporation, you're likely to take it. However, make sure that one company doesn't take up the lion's share of your bandwidth. No matter how tempting it is to have a single Fortune 500 client be your major source of income, it's just a bad plan. First of all, they're not likely to let it happen. Second, it's a good way to go out of business if something should happen on their end, or in the economy, to change your position with them.

No matter how secure you may feel, you're always wise to make sure you've spread your business across at least three major clients. Make sure you don't have more than about 30-35% of your business with any one company so, if that business is lost, you don't go down with that piece of your company. Ideally, you should have your business spread across a good range of clients, both large and small, so that you're receiving payments at net 30, net 60, net 90, net 120, etc. As larger corporations pay on later terms, you need to have business with companies that compensate you regularly so that you can pay your employees and bills on time.

Actually, many major corporations have a policy of not allowing their suppliers, especially their smaller suppliers, to do more than 30-40% of their business with the company, to protect them from failing. No matter how good a supplier you are, no matter how good your products or services are, you can only go so far and do so much. But this policy keeps your company protected and profitable. You are wise to administer this same policy to the suppliers who do business with you.

When you're just starting out, that first contract may constitute all your business. But get to work and get another deal with another company right away so that you're not vulnerable. Your contract with a major corporation is proof that you can do work with the big boys.

June Davis was just starting out in 2004. One of the large accounting firms asked her to do a training program for their women's networking, and she worked hard to do a fantastic job for them. She did extensive research, spent months preparing, and, when she went to New York, had two programs lined up. She was a huge hit, and she was hired for more work. For a few months, this was the only major corporation she had as a client.

When she spoke to other Fortune 500 corporations, she presented herself as someone who had a client list that included this big accounting firm. She didn't say that it was the only big company she had, just that it was one of her customers. The tactic worked perfectly. From that one firm, she has built a list of more than fifty Fortune 500 clients in six years.

Be sure that you protect your business by growing it wisely. Grow it across multiple companies so that you have streams of income that support you from different sources. Build a strategy that ensures that you are protecting your investment in your corporation's future, its people and profits. Many major corporations will work with you to help you grow your company with them. Find out how.

Matchmakers

If you are scheduled to meet with representatives from procurement or an SD professional at either a corporate or Council event, congratulations! Here is where you have a chance to go into more depth about your company and create more interest and excitement about your capabilities and skills.

Above all, here is where your advance research will shine, and it's critical that you come to this meeting with everything lined out about where you fit. You will usually have between ten and twenty minutes during a typical matchmaker, so use your time wisely. You want to present your case quickly and succinctly by making that fine first impression as we have already discussed. You will need to clarify the one product that you're going to present to this company as your top offering and that's going to be your value proposition; your capability statement will be built around that offering as well.

Get some initial reaction. Then, avoid making the mistake that Debbie Lumpkin, Manager of Supplier Development for Southern California Edison, describes: "Suppliers then launch into all kinds of detail about all kinds of aspects of their business that have nothing to do with what they just presented. It ruins the first impression. What they need to do is have five or six clear, crisp, well-defined bullet points for discussion that are right in line with what they presented—all right on track, on point, so that we stay on discussion. That's what works."

This will take up the bulk of your time, but not all of it. Leave time for the other person to ask you clarifying questions. Don't overwhelm with information. Most of us think that we need to over-present and that others need to know much more than they really do. Less is more in these cases. Pare down your information to the essentials. Leave plenty of breathing room and time for them to think between your points. Then let them ask for more from you, and you should ask for next steps for your close. Don't leave without asking how you see them using your product or service, where there might be a fit, or what the next step is? Leave with an action step of some kind so that you know what to do, even if it's simply to stay in touch with your SD professional. Don't leave with a nicety. And don't be afraid to ask for, but do not expect to leave with, a contract. You won't. You will, if you are fortunate, however, leave with a next step if there is a match for what you are offering.

Don't walk into these matchmaker meetings without having practiced. You think you know how long ten minutes is. Believe me, you don't. You will want to talk too much, and it will take control and confidence to slow down and deliver a practiced, professional presentation that allows you to have a good exchange. Inexperienced suppliers spend too much time on features, overwhelm their listeners, and leave without next steps. Don't be a rookie. Remember, these people have seen it all, and it's a pleasure to work with someone who takes their sensibilities into consideration.

About the Competition

No matter how you may feel or think about your competition, never, ever trash them. That means *never*. Don't stoop to that level. It can backfire, your reputation can suffer, and it can lead people to wonder what you say about them behind their backs. We are all doing our best in this tough world, and we all do what we can to compete. No matter how dastardly the deeds the other guy may be pulling, always resist the temptation to say anything negative to your client. They may be close friends, for all you know; it may be his or her kid running that business. You cannot take the chance.

When it comes time to compare yourself, do your research, be thorough, and *be factual.* No one can argue with facts. That keeps you honest and honorable. You may be asked your opinion off the record; if you answer, you are taking your chances. The wiser man or woman keeps their own counsel.

There is no gain in personal attacks. Be gracious in all your dealings. What you say gets back to those you talk about. You may end up needing a partnership with that company someday. How are you going to start that conversation if you wasted them to your Fortune 500 clients for five years?

The best you can do is your finest work and always speak highly of everyone. This is the best kind of reputation to have in any business.

Show Your Expertise

Dave Nelson, CPM, the godfather of supply chain whose mentees are now the global vice presidents of supply chains in a number of the world's largest companies, has many a story to tell about suppliers and what to do and what not to do. Here's a perfect example from Dave:

"DuPont furnished a small amount of plastic resins for plastics parts Deere used, like hoods for tractors and like that, and one day the SVP of DuPont sales wanted to have a meeting with me. My eyes glassed over, and I was not very interested in seeing him and listening to another sales pitch, but being such a good guy, after weeks, I finally gave in and had the meeting with him. That meeting knocked my socks off.

"This guy had done his research, a lot of it. As just one example, he said his competitors had sold John Deere new plastic resin compounds that sounded like they had something special about them. But they did not, and he had the data all laid out to prove it. He said we specify almost one hundred different compounds when we actually only needed thirteen and that he wanted to show some samples they had made up, tested—and he was correct. To make a long story short, DuPont saved between 30 and 40% of our resin costs, which was tens of millions of dollars, and became our major resin supplier."

When you sit down in your matchmaker, how well prepared are you? Are you ready to blow their socks off like this guy did? This goes back to research: knowing your customer, your industry, your product and service, and how you can make a difference. Imagine the size of the contract this SVP was able to win for DuPont with this sale and the ongoing revenues for his company. This is the kind of hard work and savvy it takes to play with the Fortune 500, and the higher up the Tiers you go, the more sophisticated the selling gets.

Words They Love to Hear

SD professionals need to know from suppliers that they understand that relationships and contracts take time. That they are grateful for the opportunities that Supplier Diversity presents them and that they appreciate the work that they do for MWBEs, veterans, and small businesses. It might be appropriate to mention your awareness that many SD professionals are an office of one in a very large corporation, answering thousands of phone calls from thousands of suppliers. And that many of those suppliers can be rude, aggressive, angry, demanding , impatient, and worse. These SD professionals have to sell the idea of using MWBEs and veterans to internal buyers who can be resistant at best and totally against it at worst. They get blamed for not doing enough when they are doing their best. And still the SD professional advocates in their favor for contracts.

It also might be nice to say:

> *"I'm patient."*
>
> *"I appreciate the chance to bid."*
>
> *"Thanks for your hard work on my behalf."*
>
> *"I know you'll get back to me when you can." (Then do the calling anyway.)*
>
> *"I'm grateful for the opportunity."*
>
> *"Let me know what I can do to make this easier for you."*

Sometimes when suppliers desperately want their business to succeed, they forget that the people who are working in their favor also have challenges. It's not all about you. There are thousands of suppliers just like you, many of whom have the same products and services as you, who also want those contracts. When you show respect for the hard work that SD professionals put forth in your favor, patience for the process, and regard for the people in these corporations, you will have a far greater chance of getting the business. A little humility goes a long way.

Staying in Touch

Delphi's John Taylor believes that suppliers have a responsibility to stay in touch with SD professionals, and he offers a formula for how to do it. For example, when you call him, there's specific information to leave on his voice mail. His recommendations are an excellent template for other SD professionals as well.

Taylor says, "I tell suppliers all the time that they should stay in regular contact with me—for me, 'regular' is every six to ten weeks.

"When they call, they don't have to speak to me live (that's a bonus), but they should:

1. Remind me who they are, where we met, or the last time that we spoke.

2. Give a quick update on positive changes since we last spoke:

    a. New business won or bid on

    b. New hires

    c. New certifications

    d. Acquisitions

    e. Any other very significant corporate update relevant to our business

3. They should again state their value proposition and how their products and services can benefit my company.

"This approach is information-driven, nonintrusive, and it keeps the supplier top-of-mind. Those suppliers who use this approach effectively nearly always have quote opportunities from me, or referrals to my colleagues."

It is your responsibility to stay in touch with Taylor, not Taylor's responsibility to track you down. MWBEs and veterans are the ones who must keep themselves top-of-mind, and that means staying in touch, and making it personal. Please note here that he didn't say send a text, an email, or a letter. He said *leave a message*. This may vary with other SD professionals, so be sure to ask them how they prefer for you to communicate.

Your Business Plan... Create a New Vision

Do you have a business plan? When's the last time you looked at it? When you first started your company or got a loan? Last year or ten years ago? Chances are you may not have one at all, that it's woefully outdated or gathering dust on a back shelf.

Your business plan should be a living, breathing document. It should inform your business every day. It should be a source of guidance for strategy and ideas during off moments. Something you can pull up on your computer or iPhone to remind you of where you said you were going to be right now, and where you really are, and what you still need to do to get there.

Most of us need to drastically revamp our business plans if only for one reason: we never planned to *partner*. This is the one strategic step that we must all take into account if we're going to grow organically, be able to contribute to this economy, and make a better living for ourselves, our employees, and our loved ones.

We are more likely to do what we plan, and when we rewrite our business plans, we make it real. So take out that hoary old document that started up your firm and rewrite your strategy; plan to joint venture. Imagine the perfect partner. Who would you like to work with? Who would make an ideal collaborator for you? This is where it starts to be fun. Think about who you already know out there in your business universe. Who do you admire? Who do you respect and look up to already? Whose partnership could make your business prosper even more and, more importantly, how can they benefit by working with you? How will you help them prosper?

Craft your new business plan to make it exciting and inspiring so that you'll be motivated to do it. Joint ventures are intended to be temporary, at least initially. You never know where they may take your company. Your firm could head off in a brand-new direction by the end of the year because you took a new risk, and the partnership you formed blossomed into a new corporation unimaginable six months prior. By sitting down now, and taking a few hours to create a new vision, you open up a world of possibilities for yourself and the people who count on you.

This is not the time to think small. An entire country is counting on you to imagine a company without boundaries. Think like Disney—*imagineer* something wonderful, and who your potential partners could be. Tomorrow, anything and everything could happen when you walk out the door with an open mind. It is on the backs of small businesses like you—minorities, women, veterans—that America grows and evolves and prospers. You can do this.

Your Finances

When you want to do business with a major corporation, they're going to want to know how strong you are financially. It stands to reason. They don't want to start counting on you as a supplier and then find out too late you are having financial challenges. How strong *are* you financially? Is this a strength of yours as a CEO, as a manager of your business? Or is this an area where you need help?

While you don't need to be a financial expert, you do need to be able to read your company's profit and loss statements and all the other major reports that tell how your company is faring. If finances aren't your strong point, bring into your closest circle someone you absolutely trust—an individual or a financial firm that can advise you, provide you with regular reports, and help you manage your company's financials. You must have a Dun & Bradstreet number, and it's also wise to manage your D&B credit rating, as that's a number that many companies check to see how you are rated before doing business with you.

Loans are important to establish a credit history. Many small firms, especially those started by women, pay all their bills right away and on time. While this is admirable, it doesn't build up your credit history. You must at some point take out a business loan at a reputable institution, even a small loan, just to establish some kind of payment history. This allows you to show you can manage your finances. Over time, you can take out and pay off larger loans, which will eventually come in very handy when you get bigger and need sizable funds. Someday you may want to buy another company, for example, and to do this you have to have a significant credit history. The small amount you invest in paying interest to the bank will pay off handsomely when you start playing at higher levels.

Whatever you do, make sure that you have a banker who knows you and that you have experts who know your business, do your taxes, and can provide legal assistance. The bigger you get, the more important these services are. Don't fool yourself: even if you are a one-woman or one-man business, you need a "board of directors" (see next chapter), and that means accounting and legal help.

Your Supporting Cast

When tennis star Serena Williams started playing tennis, she already had plenty of coaching. And she continued to get plenty of coaching to keep her sharp and competitive. Just because she was born with raw talent meant nothing. It's constant practice, training, and challenge that made her a champion.

A first-round draft pick NFL quarterback who joins the Baltimore Ravens is going to get a quarterback coach along with the team's head coach, and probably a lot more than that, to make sure that the multi-million-dollar deal that the team signed with him pays off. He will be coached all summer, all season, all year long, and all of his professional career. It never ends. Being a skilled athlete is just the beginning. He needs constant feedback and training to take his skills down the field to the goal line, and eventually to help his team win the Super Bowl.

It's the same on the training field of business. You are challenged every day to be the best you can be. And just like an athlete you have to reach inside to find your best. Why would you try to do that without professional guidance and training to help you be your best?

Business coaches come in many forms, and they are trained to help you set goals, run your business more effectively, reach beyond your limitations, take your firm to the next level, and, above all, get you out of your own way to make better decisions in both your personal and professional lives. Investing in a business coach can make all the difference. The same thing works for your personal life—by investing in a personal trainer. If you've let your physical health slide, you can't be your best if you're overweight or your health is poor.

You might even think about finding a personal guide, a spiritual "coach" to help you get more balance in your life. Whatever your belief system, it's key to have a higher purpose that gives your work meaning.

Does this sound like a lot? Surprisingly, it's not. When you surround yourself with people who are invested in your health, your business success, and your personal welfare and happiness, that's a great "board of directors." Whether these are people you are paying or not makes no difference. The point is that this is a support system that wants to see you succeed. These are people who won't listen to your excuses, and who will be there for you every step of the way.

Why have you resisted coaching? Ask yourself: *Does the house have to be clean before the housekeeper gets there?* If so, then you have some serious rethinking to do about how you run your household. It's time to let people be of service to you.

Think of how differently you might live your life if you had a community of people behind you. You can, starting right away. Ask around. Many people in your world are already working with coaches. Ask for a referral, and start finding out why so many people are using them. You will wonder why it took you so long to give yourself this amazing gift.

Time to Give Back

As you grow, learn, and develop, it's time for you to start giving back. Through Councils, chambers, universities, and other sources, you will meet people like you who are just starting out. You will discover many opportunities to help people using your knowledge, ideas, and know-how. Show others how to get started, how to find funding. Teach what you know: how to start a new business. Show them how to network, meet people in corporations, how to open doors. Introduce them to senior people and create business opportunities for others. Coach and mentor. As you mentor, you will learn a great deal more than you ever thought you would.

The more you give, the more you get. The more you give, the more your reputation will grow in ways you can't anticipate. But don't do it for that reason. Do it because it's the right thing to do. Because it's your turn to give back and because others need your expertise. And because there's plenty of business to go around.

The future of this country depends on the success of minority, women, and veteran businesses. The more you help, the more you ensure America's success—and the more success you will enjoy as you give.

Tackling the Titans Success Checklist

- Identify your niche

- Research, research research!

- Register on the websites of the companies where you are a fit

- Create your Seven Second Value Proposition

- Create your 15 Second Capability Statement

- Practice, practice, practice!

- Plan who you're going to meet if you're attending a conference

- Bring collateral to show only, have it ready in virtual form

- Always have plenty of business cards

- Attend every event you can: be visible, active and a leader

- Follow up with courtesy, regard and respect

- Get coaching

- Have a healthy, living business plan that plans for partnerships

- Plan to give back in multiple ways to your community

About the Author

Julia Hubbel is an award-winning entrepreneur, international professional speaker, seminar leader, and prize-winning journalist specializing in the art of communications and charisma.

Julia is a disabled, decorated Vietnam-era veteran who served as a journalist and television producer-director in the U. S. Army, and Chief of Military Protocol for the Jimmy Carter Presidential Inaugural in 1977.

In 1983, Julia hitchhiked solo around Australia, New Zealand, and the Fiji Islands, learned how to fly ultralights, and scuba dived in the Great Barrier Reef. Among her many adventures, she has explored the great animal parks of Botswana, dived with Great White sharks, and traveled to other far-flung nations such as Thailand to learn languages and cultures. She has skydived 131 times and flown base on a twelve-man star skydiving formation. She is a bodybuilder and cyclist, and an avid football fan.

In 1997, Julia created a diverse network of top-level professional women in the American Inland Northwest, using her model for establishing relationships. The Hubbel Group became a voice for professional women from all backgrounds and spun off companies, partnerships, and lasting friendships. The remarkable story of The Hubbel Group is profiled in the best-selling book *Networking Magic,* by authors Rick Frishman and Jill Lublin.

She has spent nearly three decades in senior corporate and consulting positions in the areas of training and organizational development in America, Australia, and New Zealand. Her clients include Southwest Airlines, Southern California Edison, Archer Daniels Midland, Intel, Chevron, Hewlett Packard, Bank of America, Delphi, Cisco Systems, Qwest, Schering Plough, MassMutual, Sodexo, Lockheed Martin, Pfizer and Tyco.

Julia holds a Bachelor of Science degree in Communications and Public Relations from American University in Washington, D.C. She earned her certificate as a Supplier Diversity Professional in 2008.

Her first book, *WordFood: How We Feed or Starve Our Relationships,* was published in September 2010. *WordFood* is a self-help guide on improving the diet of language we use that affects the people in our lives every day.

Bring Julia Hubbel and
Tackling the Titans
to your Organization!

Transform how your suppliers sell to the Fortune 500 and Tier One companies through Julia Hubbel's powerful books and accompanying programs. *Tackling the Titans* is available as a workshop or half-day seminar. You can order books by contacting us today. Discount rates for large orders.

We offer seminars, workshops, and coaching services for corporations and suppliers.

To schedule a call or program, please contact us at 720 221 7335.

Other programs and books by Julia Hubbel:

WordFood is also available in book form and taught in workshops. *WordFood* is the diet of language that nurtures ourselves and others every day. Learn how the words you choose affect all the people in your life: your spouse, children, friends, coworkers, customers, clients, even strangers. You'll learn to fix broken relationships, achieve greater intimacy and influence and avoid misunderstandings and arguments. Leave everyone you meet feeling nourished and encouraged.

Quick Order Form

The Hubbel Group Inc.
PO Box 27352
Lakewood, CO 80227

Tackling the Titans: *How to Sell to the Fortune 500* by Julia E. Hubbel

Three ways to order this book:
1. Telephone: 720-221-7335
2. Write to us at the address above
3. Email: jhubbel@principlednetworking.com

Pricing:
$13.95 per book, plus $4.99 shipping and handling for the first book plus $1.25 per additional books.

Colorado residents add 8% sales tax

WordFood: *How We Feed or Starve Our Relationships*, is also available at $24.95 for the first book ordered. For each additional book, add $1.25 per book for shipping and handling.

Please note: bulk pricing is available for both books. Please call us for details.

Quantity		Item Cost	Amount Due
_____	*Tackling the Titans* $13.95	$ _____	$ _____
_____	*WordFood* $24.95	_____	_____

Shipping and Handling $4.99 + $1.25 per additional book _____

Colorado residents add 8% sales tax _____

TOTAL $ _____

Payment: Make checks payable in U.S. dollars to The Hubbel Group Inc. and mail to the address above, or call us at 720-221-7335 with your credit card. We gladly accept Visa and Mastercard.

Complete your shipping information below

Name _____

Address_____

City _____ State _____ Zip_____

Phone_____

Email _____

Books will be mailed directly from the printer to you.

Thank you for your order!

CPSIA information can be obtained at www.ICGtesting.com
Printed in the USA
BVOW040726010812

296742BV00002B/1/P